In Lambeth

A Play by

Jack Shepherd

METHUEN DRAMA

A Methuen New Theatrescript

First published in Great Britain in 1990 by Methuen Drama,
Michelin House, 81 Fulham Road, London SW3 6RB

Copyright © 1990 Jack Shepherd

A CIP catalogue record for this book is available from
the British Library

ISBN 0-413-63590-2

Typeset by Hewer Text Composition Services, Edinburgh
Printed and bound in Great Britain by
Cox & Wyman Ltd, Cardiff Road, Reading

The illustration on the front cover is Plate 14 from
the Book of Urizen *by William Blake and is reproduced*
from A Large Book of Designs, *c.1794–6, by*
courtesy of the Trustees of the British Museum.

Caution

In Lambeth

'**Jack Shepherd**'s stimulating portrait of William Blake and his revolutionary near-contemporary, Thomas Paine.'

Financial Times

William Blake, the poet and artist, was born in London in 1757. He became an apprentice engraver at the age of 14 and remained poor throughout his life. He believed fervently in the revolution of the inner man, that only personal salvation and spiritual regeneration could achieve a better world, fearing that social revolution would only replace one tyranny with another. Blake died in 1827, singing hymns of joy. Thomas Paine, the political thinker and revolutionary, was born 20 years before Blake, in Thetford, Norfolk. An active figure in both the American and French revolutions, in England he was considered a traitor and in 1791 fled across the channel to France. After a period of imprisonment during 'The Terror' (1793–4), he returned to America, where he died in 1809, reviled by the Christian fundamentalists for what they saw as the profanity of his beliefs.

'**Shepherd** has crafted an enthralling confrontation that superbly sustains the delicate balance between the self-effacing nuts-and-bolts humanism of Paine and the vulnerable, fiery politics of Blake. A rare treat.'

James Christopher, *Independent*

Jack Shepherd was born in Leeds in 1940. He studied art at King's College, Newcastle, but realised the difficulties of earning a living as a painter and enrolled at the Central School of Speech and Drama in 1962. He was a student founder of the Drama Centre and since then has enjoyed a successful career as an actor, being closely associated with the Royal Court in the 1960s and the National Theatre in the 1980s. He began devising plays for the theatre in 1969, with a production of **The Incredible Journey of Sir Francis Younghusband** at the Theatre Upstairs. This was followed by **The Sleep of Reason** (Traverse Theatre, 1973), **Real Time** (Joint Stock, 1982) and **Revelations** (Bridge Lane Theatre, 1983). **In Lambeth** is his first written work for the stage, although he has written several television plays, including **Underdog** (BBC, 1978) and **Clapperclaw** (BBC, 1980). He is currently working on a shortened version of **In Lambeth** for BBC television, to be screened towards the end of 1990.

Methuen New Theatrescripts series offers frontline intelligence of the most original and exciting work from the fringe:

authors in the same series

Preface

I first saw Blake's little coloured engravings for *The Songs of Innocence* at infant school, pinned to the wall of one of the classrooms. I tried not to look at them and shuddered if I did. I encountered them again on the walls of one of the rooms of the chapel I attended as a child. Later, at grammar school, my art teacher *insisted* that I study Blake. I became fascinated. I didn't get acquainted with Tom Paine, however, until much later. Thirty years later, in fact, when I was at the National Theatre and thinking about the possibility of devising a play about his life. I wrote out several scenarios. They were very long. Too long. The canvas would have to be *too* broad, I thought, to accommodate sixty years or so of English history *and* the revolutions of America and France, so I gave up. The project was dropped.

There was, however, one scene which stayed in my imagination. It wouldn't go away. It took place in the back garden of the Blakes' cottage in Lambeth, 2a Hercules Buildings: Blake and his wife are sitting on the branch of a tree. They have been reading *Paradise Lost*. There's a full moon, low in the evening sky. And outside this little oasis, Tom Paine hurries through the dirty streets, past burning piles of rubbish, gibbets and mobs of angry men, eventually stumbling almost by accident into the Blakes' garden.

It seemed to me that a whole play might be written around this one scene, loosely based on Blake's proposition that 'opposition is true friendship'. I wrote about ten pages or so and sent them to Partisan Theatre in January of this year, saying that if they liked the idea, I'd try and finish it. They wrote back to say that if I'd finish it, they'd put it on! Thanks largely to their encouragement and energy, the play was performed at the East Dulwich Tavern in the summer of 1989. By a wonderful coincidence, we opened on the night of the bicentenary of the storming of the Bastille.

In Lambeth was first performed at the Dulwich Tavern on 12 July 1989, and then at the Donmar Warehouse, directed by Jack Shepherd and designed by Jake Shepherd. The cast was as follows:

William Blake	Michael Maloney
Catherine Blake	Lesley Clare O'Neill
Tom Paine	Bob Peck

Other parts were played by Andrew Calloway

A garden belonging to a small cottage: in Lambeth.

It is some time ago, but the sense of period should not be overstated. The grass is uncut. The flowerbeds are overgrown, profuse with weeds and vegetables. A high brick wall separates the garden and the street. There is a doorway through to the street – stage right. A door through to the kitchen – stage left. A vine grows up one side of the house.

It is late in the day. A large full moon rides in the evening sky. A few indigo clouds near the horizon.

In the corner of the garden is an oak tree. There are two naked figures sitting on one of the branches. A man and a woman. They are sitting with their backs to us. The man is playing on a tin whistle. He stops abruptly in mid phrase, seeing someone in the highest branches of the tree.

Blake Didn't you like it? I'm surprised . . . Well, you taught it to me . . . No, not in that key, I'll admit . . . I can only really play this in one key – 'C' – I think . . . And I've never been able to transpose . . . I do wish you wouldn't come here in the evenings. It's most intimidating. Especially when I'm trying to practise.

He stares for a few seconds, quite still.

Blake I don't like you standing behind me! Your wings are glinting in the sun!

Mrs Blake (*after a pause*) Is it Gabriel again?

Blake *shakes his head.*

Mrs Blake Raphael?

Blake I don't know his name.

Mrs Blake (*whispering*) Why don't you ask?

Blake He wasn't over keen on my playing. I'm afraid he might take offence and throw something at me.

Mrs Blake (*worried*) What?

Blake I don't know. A brick or something.

Mrs Blake Shouldn't we be getting down now? It's nearly dark.

Blake Wait till he goes.

Mrs Blake Yes . . . I suppose it might seem a bit rude . . . What's he like, this one? Is he naked?

Blake Yes. He has a face like an Assyrian . . . like a *king* of the Assyrians! His eyes are blue and his dark hair falls in ringlets half way down his back.

Mrs Blake He sounds beautiful . . . can *I* see him?

Blake Don't get carried away. For one thing, angels don't have genitals. They don't need them any more. They're above that sort of thing. That's the whole point.

Mrs Blake Where is he anyway?

Blake He's standing on your head.

Mrs Blake *gives a little scream, then looks up – as if there really was someone standing on her head – brushing her hair with a scatterbrained flapping motion. She calms.*

Mrs Blake Whenever you're in a mood, you behave like this . . . Why can't you lose your temper like other people? Act normal for once. Instead of all this . . . *distraction*! Sometimes I wonder about you.

Blake Well, you know what they say don't you?

Mrs Blake What?

Blake About me . . .

Mrs Blake Yes, I know what they say. But they're wrong. It's not *that*! It's –

Blake Look! (*Points.*) There he goes . . .

Mrs Blake It's like I'm seeing you through broken glass.

Blake (*he stares into the setting sun, eyes creased up. Then suddenly, he waves*) Bye . . .

Pause.

Mrs Blake He wasn't really standing on my head was he? I mean, not really?

Blake Oh yes.

Pause.

Mrs Blake I'll make some tea.

Blake Tea . . .

Mrs Blake I bought some tea.

Blake Did you?

Mrs Blake It comes from India, you know. They import it in great big boxes. You can see them stacked up at the back of the shop. They're handy for storing things.

Blake I thought tea came from China.

Mrs Blake Not the tea I bought.

Blake There is a tea that comes from China. I know because a Chinaman once told me all about it.

Mrs Blake I've never seen a Chinaman.

Blake I met him on the Walworth Road. On a Saturday. He was wearing a large broad-brimmed hat. Made out of straw. He wanted to know the way to the Elephant and Castle. He said his name was Wang. I think, in *spirit*, he was the emanation of an emperor, from the days of the Tang Dynasty.

Pause.

Mrs Blake I once saw a black man at Camberwell market. He was eating fire. He'd put a burning stick in his mouth and breathe out flames, like a dragon.

Blake When was this?

Mrs Blake A long time ago . . . I was only a girl. There was a dwarf running round collecting money, I remember. In a loin cloth and a bright green turban with silver stars sewn on it. I was frightened. I think everyone was. When they'd finished I watched them sharing out the money. They were resting in this old tent. The black man had burned himself. He kept rinsing out his mouth and spitting on the grass. I noticed

that people shied away from him. I think because of his colour.
I was only little don't forget. I thought he was black because
he got burned every day by the flames . . .

(**Blake** *laughs quietly.*)

Mrs Blake Don't laugh at me.

Blake I'm not.

Mrs Blake You *are*!

Blake No I'm not.

Mrs Blake (*after a pause*) You *were* laughing at me. Not out
loud, that's true. But you were *inside*. I could see it in your
eyes.

Blake I was just thinking what a beautiful and innocent child
you must've been.

Mrs Blake It's no use trying to get round me. Anyway, now
I come to think of it, the man in the shop said there'd been
a lynching.

Blake What?

Mrs Blake I think it was last night. Or it may have been the
night before.

Blake Where was this?

Mrs Blake In Catford apparently.

Blake Catford?

Mrs Blake Yes. There's conflicting stories about it. Someone
was saying that he'd been caught looting. But the man in the
shop said it was really because he was a republican. He said
they'd pinned a piece of paper to his chest which said: 'Death
to Lafayette', and then they'd strung him up. 'We're going to
string 'em all up!' the man in the shop said. 'All the *Frenchies*!
All the republican scum!'

Blake Was he referring to me do you think?

Mrs Blake You're a poet. You don't count.

He laughs.

Blake And since I'm a poet, I don't constitute a *threat*. Is that what you mean?

Mrs Blake No you don't, thank goodness.

Blake Well, not *physically* that's true. But what about *spiritually*?

Mrs Blake How can you threaten anyone spiritually? I don't understand.

Blake I have subversive ideas.

Mrs Blake Do you?

Blake Oh yes.

Mrs Blake Then why hasn't your work been banned?

Blake Because it hasn't been read! That's why! I mean by the people for whom it was intended! . . . 'The people!'

Mrs Blake What people!

Blake *The* people! The thing is, before they can *read* it they've got to be able to *read*!

Mrs Blake They think you're a crank.

Blake A madman. In other countries, dissidents are very properly executed. Not so here. In England we're considered eccentric . . . and very improperly . . . ignored.

Mrs Blake And ridiculed, William.

Blake That too. . . . When the prophetic voice is silenced, terrible things happen. . . . Look at the biblical evidence. The 'Book of Job' for example . . . (*He looks up into the sky.*)

> Rintrah roars and shakes his fires in the burdened air, hungry clouds swag on the deep . . .

Pause. **Blake** *looks at his wife, as if expecting her to agree.*

Mrs Blake Are you talking to me?

Blake Who did you think I was talking to?

Mrs Blake I don't know. Most of the time, I suppose, I assume you're talking to me. But I'm never really sure.

Blake Does that make you unhappy?

Mrs Blake No, not unhappy. Let's get down now. I'm getting cold.

Blake Something's the matter though, isn't it? What is it? You can tell *me*.

He gets close to her and peers into her face.

Mrs Blake I get a bit tired sometimes. That's all.

Blake What else?

Mrs Blake It's just so hard keeping up with you. (*She attempts a smile.*) Sometimes, when I'm out there in the street, shopping, whenever we've the money, which God knows isn't often, I sometimes find myself looking through the windows of other people's houses . . . and thinking that life could be so much *easier* . . . that's all. . . . We're not like any other man and wife I know! (*She bites her lip.*) It's so bloody difficult, isn't it?

Blake That's right. It's damn bloody blasted difficult! Fucking cunting difficult! But I'll tell you what. Life *here* is a damn sight better than where we were before! Eh? Better than the fucking centre of bloody London eh? Here I can sit naked in my own fucking tree in my own bastard garden even when it's pissing down and what cunt is going to stop me! No more fucking sniggering from behind the blasted windows! No more fucking complaining from the powers that fucking well be! And no more fucking interference from the damn and blasted bloody agents of the shit bag bloody bastards . . . (*He finally runs out of steam.*)

Mrs Blake Steady on. (*Pause.*) You're always better after a good rant, aren't you William?

Blake 'Damn braces. Bless relaxes . . .' (*He puts an arm round her.*) It doesn't do to get too carried away though, does it?

Blake That depends. (*She puts a hand on his knee.*) With some things . . . it's good to get carried away isn't it? And there again . . . with other things . . . (*She removes her hand.*) It's not.

She stands, picks up her hat and prepares to descend the tree.

Blake Why did you bring the hat?

Mrs Blake In case the sun got in my eyes when I was reading.

Blake It suits you.

She picks up a book. Paradise Lost.

Mrs Blake Give over.

Blake It looks so delightfully unnecessary.

Mrs Blake It's no use getting ideas.

Blake Why not?

Mrs Blake It's not possible up here.

Blake I wouldn't say that.

Mrs Blake Not anymore it isn't. If it ever was.

Blake Oh, it would have been at one time I assure you. We have happily copulated, have we not, in the most extraordinary and unpropitious places? And often with the most unexpectedly pleasurable results.

Mrs Blake True . . . you always were an athlete, Mr Blake.

A hunched figure scurries on to the stage through the outer door. He has been running. He is out of breath. Frightened, but well able to control the panic. He looks back towards the road, listening, as if he might be being followed. He relaxes. Looks briefly towards the garden and knocks on the back door.

Blake There's someone at the door.

Mrs Blake We'd better go down . . .

Blake I suppose we had . . .

They descend. The **Stranger** *knocks again on the door.*

Mrs Blake Coo-ee! We're coming . . . Won't be a minute.

Stranger (*staring myopically into the gloom*) Is there someone there? I can't see very clearly . . . I'm trying to find the whereabouts of a Mr and Mrs Blake.

Two naked shadowy figures approach him from across the lawn.

Blake Yes – that's us.

Stranger Good. Good. I've been asking everywhere . . . no one seemed to know where you lived.

Blake (*offering his hand*) How do you do.

Stranger How do you do. . . . And you must be Mrs Blake I presume. (*He takes her hand.*) I really am very pleased to meet you both. Allow me to introduce myself, I'm –

Blake Yes?

Stranger But you're – you're both – you're both not –

Blake Not what?

Stranger Not not – excuse me, but I've never seen a –

Mrs Blake What's the matter?

Stranger It's just your lack of . . . any sort of . . . I mean I hadn't really expected it, that's all. . . . In this every day sort of circumstance. What I'm saying is that I'm not yet so *inured* to the spectacle, to the *sudden* spectacle of . . . *bareness* . . . that I am able to stand before it, as it were . . . before *you* rather . . . without, a certain trepidation.

Blake Pity.

Stranger Yes, I suppose it is really.

Blake You obviously didn't go to art school.

Stranger No.

Pause.

Stranger I was a customs officer.

Blake And in such an occupation people, on the whole, are inclined to keep their clothes *on*, are they not?

Stranger They are, yes.

Awkward pause.

Stranger It is, after all, a position of trust.

Mrs Blake Don't mind him, Mr –

Stranger Paine.

Mrs Blake Mr Paine . . . it's just his way . . .

Paine *stares at them.*

Blake You wouldn't be Mr *Thomas* Paine, would you, of Thetford?

Paine That's me.

Blake We'll put our clothes on.

Paine No no . . . if that's what you prefer. You stay as you are . . . don't mind me. . . . Who am I to . . . er insist on . . . propriety?

Blake Are you offering to join us, Mr Paine?

Paine I hardly think I've known you long enough, Mr Blake. Besides, the evening air is just a little too cool for a man of my years.

Paine *is in his mid fifties.* **Blake** *in his early thirties.*

Blake I'm inclined to agree with you . . . I'm far from warm myself.

Mrs Blake Shall we go indoors?

Blake Very well . . .

He reaches down and picks up a pile of discarded clothes: breeches, a white shirt stained with ink, buckle shoes.

Blake If you'd go through there, Mr Paine, my wife will show you into the sitting room.

Paine Thank you.

Paine *and* **Mrs Blake** *go in.*

Blake I won't be a moment.

Blake *starts to change, whistling to himself. After a few moments he turns to the audience.*

Blake Hello. You mustn't think that we make a habit of this sort of thing – throwing off our clothes whenever the sun comes out – and entertaining strangers without a stitch on, and so on. . . . The climate's against it for one thing. And for most of the time, I'm afraid, the inclination just isn't there.

No . . . on the *surface*, our lives are fairly ordinary. Hum-drum. Our pleasure is very often in our work and my nature is such that for much of the time I keep no company other than my own.

Mrs Blake (*off*) William!

Blake There's a story about that. An apocryphal story. Catherine was talking to someone, *who* I don't know . . . 'And how is Mr Blake?' they enquired. 'I'm not sure,' my wife replied, 'he is so often in paradise these days'. . . . Or something like that. It's probably not even true. You know how these stories get around.

Mrs Blake (*off*) William! Hurry up!

Blake (*examines his clothes*) It's *strange* wearing clothes, isn't it? We get so used to it we lose our sense of wonder and start thinking that the clothed state is the *natural* one. Which it isn't. Besides, we look so *vulnerable* without them, like crabs without their shells. It's as if there's something missing from the original design, something that would enable us to endure the summer sun and the winter cold . . . without having to resort to these. (*Touching them.*) Layers of clothes.

Mrs Blake (*appearing at the door*) William. It's *you* he wants to talk to.

Blake I'm *serious*. Well . . . almost. The form of man is *perfect*, isn't it? (*Touching himself.*) Head. Body. Arms. Legs . . . genitals. Perfect. (*Standing as in 'Glad Day'.*) Who could seriously imagine us other than the way we are? God made us, after all, in *his* image.

Mrs Blake *goes back inside, almost bumping into* **Paine** *in the doorway.*

Paine Mr Blake . . .

Mrs Blake Excuse me.

Blake (*shaking his fist at the sky*) 'Old nobodaddy aloft . . . Farted and belched and coughed . . .'

Paine *stares at* **Blake** *for a while then goes back inside.*

Blake God isn't *up there* you know, sitting in judgement, as it were, on a cloud, with a long white beard, inventing awful rules so that people feel guilty all the time, and so on. . . . That's someone else entirely. God is *within*! It's *man* who is without. *Cosmic man!* . . . If you don't understand that, don't worry, you're in good company. Besides, you'll get the point eventually. I mean by the time you're dead . . . when your spirit will become so agile, you'll find that you can leap from star to star in a single stride.

Paine *appears in the doorway.*

Pause.

Blake There are, of course, people who would dispute that: mathematicians, philosophers, engineers like Arkwright and scientists like Newton!

Paine I couldn't help hearing –

Blake (*becoming increasingly wild in speech and manner*) Isaac bloody Newton! . . . He is a most perfect symbol of that oppressive and ruthless spirit, which is the *governing force* in our society! And an embodiment of that *cosmic* spirit, who holds our world in the direst subjugation! And who with terrible *laws* oppresses us all and sticks us down and makes us to know our bloody place! Many people worship this horrible emanation and call it God. A *good* God and a *just* one. . . . They're wrong of course. For if this *good* God were in fact *just*, as they suppose, the world he created would be *just* too. But the world *isn't* just. Society isn't just! Far from it . . .

> How the chimney sweepers cry
> Every black'ning church appalls
> And the hapless soldiers sigh
> Runs in blood down palace walls!

Paine Well said, Mr Blake.

Blake But –

Blake *just stands and stares. We don't know if he's thinking dark and profound thoughts or whether he just hates being interrupted in full flow.*

Paine Well said . . .

Blake *looks at him.* **Paine** *stares back. A kind of deadlock.*

Blake (*breaking the ice*) What? What was I saying?

Paine I'm sorry. I've made you f – You've lost your drift. That's my fault. I'm sorry.

Blake No.

Paine Yes it is. Yes it is. I'm sorry, I shouldn't've interrupted you.

Blake No no. Thoughts are elusive. You must catch a thought as it flies, trapping it briefly, inside your head, like the tiniest of birds, otherwise it might fly off, never to return. It might even die on you. (*Pause.*) Don't you agree, Mr Paine?

Paine I have never really thought of the 'intellectual processes' in that particular way, Mr Blake. Though I do recognise *something* in what you say . . . I have to admit . . . (*Smiles.*) I was never a great man for whisky, I'm afraid. . . . Whenever *my* inspiration begins to flag a bit . . . brandy has always proved extremely effective in reviving it . . . or rum . . . in rather large quantities.

Blake Brandy is bad for the liver, is it not?

Paine It is indeed . . . (*Pause.*) Though not as bad as port . . . or so I'm told . . . or absinthe.

Blake I was always of the opinion that people drank to reach oblivion.

Paine So they do, ultimately.

Blake Why is that, do you think?

Paine People wish for oblivion because, for *them*, life is hell.

Blake Their life on earth?

Paine Their *life*.

Blake And why is their life hell, Mr Paine?

Paine Because society would have it so, Mr Blake.

Blake Agreed . . .

Pause.

> But most through midnight streets I hear
> How the youthful Harlot's curse
> Blasts the newborn Infant's tear
> And blights with plagues the marriage hearse.

What is your opinion of tyranny, Mr Paine?

Paine Pretty much the same as yours, Mr Blake, I should think.

Blake Would you say *our* system was tyrannical?

Paine That would depend on how you define tyranny. Some would argue we're a free people.

Blake But not you.

Paine We have only the trappings of democracy.

Blake And not the actuality.

Paine Absolutely not. (*Pause.*) A little earlier, I heard you talking about the law and justice, or rather the lack of it. As I see it . . . all systems are despotic if they don't take into account the wishes, the needs of *all* the people. In France, before the revolution, it was the king and the people *surrounding* the king who subjugated the people, here it is the government . . . and the will of commerce. Despotism doesn't necessarily stem from an *individual person*, it spreads through the body of the state, like a cancer. It strengthens itself by assuming the appearance of duty and *tyrannises* with its repeated calls for unthinking obedience.

Blake Well said Mr Paine . . . just so. (*He smiles.*)

The tension between them has eased somewhat.

Blake (*suddenly*) Would you say there is a conspiracy against me, or is it that my work just isn't good enough?

Silence. **Paine** *is confused. He tries to say 'What' but the word doesn't come out.*

Paine W –

Blake (*going on as if the previous question had never been asked*) Have you come far?

Mrs Blake *appears in the doorway.*

Paine From Hampstead . . . I walked most of the way . . .

Blake You *did*?

Paine Yes, I don't enjoy coach journeys on bad roads. It's bad for the digestion.

Blake I agree. I much prefer walking. Kate and I often take long walks in the country. Just for the fun of it.

Paine You *do*?

Mrs Blake We once walked to Tunbridge Wells and back.

Paine In a *day*? (**Mrs Blake** *nods*.) . . . Tunbridge Wells must be 30 miles away at least!

Blake Yes.

Paine Did you have any particular reason to go to Tunbridge Wells?

Blake Not as I recall. . . . The pleasure of that particular 'expedition' was to be found more in the conception than the execution.

They laugh.

Mrs Blake As far as I'm concerned, walking is a very reliable way of getting from one place to another. It's cheap too.

Pause.

Paine It is indeed, Mrs Blake.

Mrs Blake Call me Kate, everyone else does.

Paine Right, Kate . . . Why don't you call me Tom?

Mrs Blake Tom . . .

Paine What about you . . . Mr Blake? Are you a William or a Bill?

Blake Bill to you . . . Tom.

Paine Bill then . . .

Paine *is a little more at ease now, but not entirely sure of himself.*

Mrs Blake Tom. I had a great uncle Tom. He had white hair and big watery grey eyes . . . like something from underneath the ground. . . . He'd lost a leg at Malplaquet. . . . When I knew him, he ran this gin palace in the city. Whenever there was trouble he'd unstrap his wooden leg and use it like a bludgeon. He was buried, for some reason, in a pauper's grave.

Blake Well Tom, you must be hungry after your journey. When will supper be ready, Kate?

Mrs Blake It'll be a while yet.

Blake What are we having?

Mrs Blake Rabbit pie.

Pause.

Paine I wouldn't say no to a drink.

Mrs Blake What would you like?

Blake Kate was going to make some tea, weren't you Kate?

Paine *Tea?* No thank you, much too exotic.

Mrs Blake There's some fruit juice. And water . . . We've nothing stronger, Tom, I'm afraid Bill doesn't really apr –

Blake (*cutting her short*) I'll go and get something! What would you like? Beer? Gin? Brandy? A bottle of wine? Look, I'll go down to the village. It's not far. I'll be back in five minutes.

Paine This is very embarrassing – I didn't mean –

Blake (*beaming hugely*) You're our *guest!* (*Privately to* **Mrs Blake**.) Where's the money?

Mrs Blake On the shelf by the sink.

Blake *runs inside.*

Paine I'm sorry about this.

Mrs Blake He's always been a bit on the impulsive side.

Blake (*off*) It's not there!

Mrs Blake Try the cupboard by the back door!

Blake (*off*) Got it!

Mrs Blake Leave some for tomorr –

Blake (*racing out of the door, carrying a jar with a few coins in the bottom*) I'll bring back some wine. If that's –

Mrs Blake Don't spend it all –

Blake If that's what you really want, Tom.

Paine You don't *have to* do this . . . you really don't. But, if you *insist* . . . *if* you insist . . . some wine would be very nice.

Blake Good.

Blake *races out into the street.*

Paine Only . . .

Blake (*turning in the doorway*). What?

Paine No . . . wine is perfect . . . Get a bottle of wine.

Blake You must take your pleasure as you find it, that's what I say! Mr Thomas Paine. 'The soul of sweet delight can never be defiled!'

Mrs Blake Bill, *please*!

Blake (*racing down the street*) 'The road of excess leads to the palace of wisdom!'

An awkward pause. **Mrs Blake** *feels drawn towards the kitchen.*

Mrs Blake You do like rabbit pie, don't you?

Paine (*pause*) I just love it.

Mrs Blake (*off*) There's potatoes and greens. And apple and custard.

Paine It sounds delicious. I've not had rabbit pie in a long, long time. Not since I was last in England probably.

Mrs Blake You've been away?

Paine I lived in America until a few years ago. And then France . . .

Mrs Blake (*appearing in the doorway*) America! Oh, I've always wanted to go there. What were you doing in America?

Paine Fighting the War of Independence.

Mrs Blake Really? Whose side were you on?

Paine Theirs.

Mrs Blake You were fighting against the British?

Paine Most definitely.

Mrs Blake You were a revolutionist?

Paine Of a kind.

Mrs Blake Did you kill anyone?

Paine I wasn't a terribly good soldier I'm afraid. If I killed anyone it was almost certainly by accident. I remember firing off a musket at the battle of Trenton Falls. But I wasn't at all sure in which direction I was supposed to be facing. I mean, it's perfectly feasible I could have shot at people on my own side. Thereafter I confined myself to doing what I do best. Writing articles. Pamphlets. Manifestos. To inform. To educate. To counter the lies put about by the enemy. To stir up! To rabble rouse! To keep the flame of revolution burning in the hearts of men, day by day.

Silence.

Mrs Blake Oh you're *that* Thomas Paine! I'm sorry, I didn't realise. . . . They make likenesses of you out of old bits of cloth and newspapers, and burn them on bonfire night, did you know that?

Paine I was aware of that fact. Yes.

Mrs Blake You're a public enemy . . . (**Paine** *nods*.) A bugbear . . .

Paine That's what they say.

Mrs Blake You look much too nice to be a bugbear . . . (*She smiles*.) Were you acquainted with Thomas Jefferson? (**Paine** *nods*.) And General Washington? (**Paine** *nods*.) They weren't really such *bad* people were they?

Paine In what sense, Mrs Blake?

Mrs Blake Kate.

Paine Kate then. In what sense were they 'bad' exactly?

Mrs Blake Well, if you were to believe half the things that were written about them at the time . . . I mean . . . they were supposed to be less than human and foaming at the mouth. (**Paine** *laughs*.) What's so funny?

Paine The reports were false. *Deliberately* false! Wicked inventions of the British Government! Lies and distortions, fed to the people, with the intention of creating a climate of opinion wholly *antagonistic* towards our friends over there in the colonies. In other words, Kate, they didn't want anyone over here – anyone like yourself for example – sympathising and above all *identifying* with them.

Mrs Blake Yes, that's what Bill's always said. But . . . I don't know . . . I mean . . . you don't know who to believe, do you?

Paine They were never 'bad' men, Kate, in the sense that I think you mean. But that doesn't mean to say that they were *good* men either. Necessarily. To tell the truth, Kate, I don't think many of them were cut out to be radicals. We're talking about the higher echelons, you understand, the *leadership*. . . . In my opinion, most of 'em would've been far happier running a large estate in the country . . . or managing slaves . . .

Mrs Blake Not all of them, surely. What about – ? Oh, what's his name? The one who flew a kite in a thunderstorm. What do they call him? He was over here not long ago trying to patch things up . . .

Paine Franklin? Benjamin Franklin?

Mrs Blake *Franklin!* That's his name! What about him?

Paine He's a good man, Kate. By and large. He's a scientist.

Mrs Blake Bill doesn't reckon much to scientists.

Paine No . . .

Mrs Blake Anyway . . . (*Pause.*) Fancy exchanging pleasantries with a public enemy. . . . Whatever would my father think? (*Pause.*) It just shows you, doesn't it? Why did you come here?

Long pause.

Paine I don't know exactly . . .

Mrs Blake To see Bill?

Paine Yes.

Mrs Blake But there's something else.

Paine Yes. (*Pause.*) I suppose it was in the back of my mind
. . . to pay you a visit . . . I've heard so much about you. . . .
But that wasn't the reason I came here. Not directly. No. You
see, I'd been to see a certain gentleman on the little matter of
a bridge that I've designed and not unnaturally wish to see
built. And as –

Mrs Blake A bridge?

Paine Yes, but that's all –

Mrs Blake An *iron* bridge?

Paine Yes, but that's all by the by. . . . A short while after
leaving the gentleman's house, just by the wall of Lambeth
Palace, a crowd of angry people swept by me, knocking me
down. As I got up, brushing mud from my knees. I noticed a
carriage drawing up alongside. A man leaned out. 'What's *your*
name?' he asked. I didn't reply. Not straight away. Something
in his voice put me on my guard. I looked at him. He looked
at me. *And* . . . I had the most terrible sense of unease. I
said something to him, *what*, I can't say exactly and took off
down the street, with a firm stride. Once round the corner,
I ran!

Mrs Blake Were you very frightened?

Paine I suppose I must've been. But for no clear reason. . . .
However, once I'd remembered that your house was in the
vicinity, I was drawn towards it, as an accused man is drawn
to the idea of sanctuary.

Mrs Blake Who was the man?

Paine I don't know. His face seemed familiar. But I'm not
sure. I may have seen him once before. Loitering outside my
gate. But as I say, I'm not sure.

Mrs Blake He'll be back in a minute.

Paine Who will?

Mrs Blake Bill.

Paine Ah.

Mrs Blake He'll be back with the wine.

Paine Yes.

An awkward pause. **Mrs Blake** *edges back towards the kitchen.*

Paine Have you lived here long?

Mrs Blake We haven't been here very long. Anyway it makes a change from central London. . . . It's a bit out of the way, of course. But I suppose we're rather suited to that. . . . We haven't done much to it either, not that there aren't things need doing. The roof leaks. We need new guttering. But we've been very happy here, taking things by and large.

Paine It's very nice . . . very *rustic.*

Mrs Blake Do you like the garden?

Paine It's a bit wild.

Mrs Blake That's Bill's doing. Personally I prefer a nice tidy garden. But Bill can't bear to see anything cut back. He doesn't even let me mow the grass. He says it's 'man imposing himself on nature', and he doesn't really approve of that.

Paine I see . . . Still, it has a very romantic aspect. Gothic almost . . .

Mrs Blake Gothic?

Paine Yes.

Mrs Blake That's very much in vogue at the moment isn't it? The Gothic . . . I've heard Bill's friends talking about it quite a lot recently. Not that I know what it means exactly. Bill's been filling in the gaps in my education over the past few years . . . but that's been mainly with regard to the classics . . . and mediaeval art and Milton and so on . . .

Paine You're fond of poetry then?

Mrs Blake Living with a poet you haven't really got much choice, have you?

Paine I suppose not. Does he manage to make any sort of living out of it?

Mrs Blake *Poetry.* What do you think?

Paine Probably not.

Mrs Blake It's the engraving that pays the bills. He makes engraved copies of paintings and illustrations for books. He accepts any sort of commission, you'd be surprised. I remember once, taking him his lunch, and there he was copying this painting of a woman, sprawled on a bed, wearing nothing but a ribbon tied just underneath her breasts, decorated with a little heart, placed just about here . . .

Paine But that's pornography . . . isn't it?

Mrs Blake Well, that's what I would've said. But there he was, working away quite happily, whistling to himself, as if it was a perfectly normal thing to be doing. . . . But that's him all over. He has these somewhat radical ideas about sexuality. Did you know that?

She sits down next to **Paine**.

Paine I *had* gathered that . . . I mean . . . if you'll cast your mind back to when I first came in . . . I assume there was a *philosophical* basis in the both of you . . . presenting yourself to me . . . in an unclothed state? (*Pause.*) Not that you were expecting me exactly.

Mrs Blake (*smiling*) He wrote this little poem once:

> In a wife I would desire
> What in whores is always found –
> The lineaments of gratified desire.

Paine Mm . . .

Mrs Blake He asked me once if I loved him. 'Yes,' I said, 'of course I do.' And then he said, 'That means you want me to be happy?' 'Yes,' I said, 'of course I want you to be happy.' 'But what if my happiness means sharing you with other women?' I couldn't answer him straight away. I found the idea very shocking. But somewhere at the back of my mind I was very excited by the possibility. He isn't at all possessive you know. Just the opposite in fact.

Paine I thought he was a religious man.

Mrs Blake Oh, he *is* . . . very.

Silence.

Mrs Blake It's a funny thing 'desire' isn't it? Some days there's nothing further from your mind . . . and at other times it takes you quite over . . . and you can think of nothing else.

Paine Dear Mrs Blake . . . I'm fearless when it comes to politics, and unusually eloquent on the subject. But with regard to this 'other matter' . . . I confess I'm rather at a loss. Since I first met you, *and* Mr Blake . . . a few moments ago . . . everything I've experienced has been, in some way . . . a *provocation*. I feel I'm someone else entirely . . . in a magic garden perhaps . . . under the moon of a distant star.

We hear **Blake** *singing in the distance.*

Blake
> Piping down the valleys wild,
> Piping songs of pleasant glee,
> On a cloud I saw a child,
> And he laughing said to me . . .

Mrs Blake *kisses* **Paine** *tenderly on the cheek.*

Mrs Blake You're unaccustomed to being loved, I think.

The door opens. **Paine** *starts up in a guilty fashion and walks awkwardly towards the garden.*

Blake *races in from the street.*

Blake I bought a flagon of apple wine and a small quantity of French brandy . . . knowing your predilection for the latter.

Paine Thank you. You're very kind. Overwhelmingly so.

Mrs Blake Where's the change?

Blake There isn't any.

Mrs Blake (*under her breath*) *Bill!*

Blake *runs into the kitchen.*

Paine What a beautiful evening. It's like Midsummer's eve *ought* to be, and very seldom is . . .

Blake *returns with a large glass and two smaller ones.*

Blake Sit down. Sit down.

Paine *does so. A little stiffly.* **Blake** *sets the large glass and the brandy in front of him.*

Blake Help yourself.

Blake *pours out a small amount of wine into his wife's glass and a little less into his own.*

Mrs Blake Bill, you *shouldn't* really. Strong drink goes straight to your head.

Blake I know. (*Grinning.*) That's the whole point. (*He drinks.*) We should propose a toast. That's the correct procedure is it not? On occasions like this . . .

Paine (*lifting his glass*) Here's to a better world.

Blake A better world in *our lifetime* . . .

Mrs Blake A better world for all God's children.

They drink.

Blake
>   When Adam delved and Eve span,
>   Who was then the gentleman?

Paine Is that one of yours?

Blake No no. It's traditional, as far as I know. I'm surprised you haven't heard it before. It's an age-old justification for insurrection. 'When Adam *delved* and Eve *span* who was *then* the *gentleman?*'

Paine Ah.

Blake Would you have the fabric of our society torn down, Mr Paine?

Paine With my bare hands, Mr Blake, if that were possible. And rebuilt too, so that *every man* might benefit and have a share in the government of his country.

Blake 'Rebuilt' you say . . . not just torn down?

Paine I do indeed.

Blake
>   Prisons are built with the stones of law.
>   Brothels with the bricks of religion.

That's one of mine. What do you make of that?

Paine *looks at* **Blake**. *A hint of discord. Nothing more.* **Paine** *does not press the point.* **Blake** *pours more wine, drinking it quickly.*

Mrs Blake Are you enjoying the brandy, Tom?

Paine It's quite delicious. (*Looking at the label.*) The very best.

Blake *laughs suddenly. The wine is having its effect.*

Blake When I was in the village just now, I saw a coach from the City drawing in. It was full of the usual people: Madame La-dee-dah and Monsieur Footle-pot, Sir Fa-la-lah and Bishop Gutty-fat. I watched them getting off, chattering and sneering at each other. . . . Last to disembark, however, were two men who pretty much kept their own company. Their faces were pale like the surface of the moon. Bloodless. They stood there on the cobblestones looking for all the world like carrion in search of a carcass.

Paine Who were they do you think?

Blake Agents of the Government, probably, or Bow Street runners. 'Who are you staring at?' one of them said to me, 'What's your name?' (**Blake** *reaches for the bottle, fills his glass and downs it in one.*)

Mrs Blake William!

Paine And what did you reply?

Blake 'William Blake.' What else? (*He laughs.*) Now I think of it, they had scales instead of skin, and bright green tongues that flickered in and out . . . and as I watched, they slid out of their clothes and slithered down the road on their great bellies, with a dry rattling sound, like leaves blowing in the wind.

Blake *gulps down the wine, then reaches for more.*

Mrs Blake I'm taking this inside.

Blake Don't be a spoil-sport.

Mrs Blake I'll go and see if the dinner's ready. You can have some more with your meal.

Mrs Blake *goes inside taking the wine with her.* **Blake** *checks to see that* **Mrs Blake** *isn't watching and then pours a little of the brandy into his glass.*

Blake In for a penny . . . (*Drinks.*) Strewth!

Paine   The native Indians call it 'fire-water', I believe.

Blake   'Fire-water . . .'

Paine   Yes. We introduced them to it, trading it for *land*.

Blake   *They* drink *this*?

Paine   In considerable quantity I believe.

Blake   I'm surprised there are any of them left.

Blake *pours the remainder of the brandy into* **Paine**'s *glass. He stops. Looks. He is listening intently.*

Blake   Robert? Is that you? . . . No, you're not intruding . . . we are having Mr Paine to dinner. . . . Come and join us.

Paine *strains to see who* **Blake** *is talking to.*

NOTE. This is the second time that **Blake** *is seen talking with a spirit. On the first occasion he is seen talking to an angel. But is he* actually *talking to an angel or is he just being mischievous? On this* second *occasion, there should be no ambivalence. He is talking to* **Robert**. *His dead brother.*

Blake *watches as* **Robert** *sits in the chair recently vacated by* **Mrs Blake**.

Blake   How are you, Robert? . . . Good. . . . Yes, yes I'll pass that on . . . I'll tell mother next time I see her . . . I expect she forgot . . . *she*'s the one who tidies up your grave. . . . Well I'll bring some then, next time I visit. What would you like? Primroses? Chrysanthemums? . . . Right. . . . She still loves you, Robert. We all do. It's just that she's getting old. She forgets things. . . . What? (*He looks sharply at* **Paine**. *Then very quietly.*) Where Mr Paine buys his clothes, Robert, is entirely *his* affair. It shouldn't concern you. . . . (*Louder.*) What sort of a message? . . . I see . . . (*Listens.*)

Mrs Blake (*from the doorway*)   Dinner's ready now. If you'd like to come and get it.

Blake   No, I'll tell him later. (*Muttering.*) Let him enjoy his rabbit pie.

He takes out a handkerchief and blows his nose.

We're always thinking of you, Robert. . . . All right then . . . bye . . .

Blake *watches him go. The atmosphere is quiet and sad.*

Blake (*to* **Mrs Blake**) Robert was here again.

Mrs Blake Yes, I realised . . .

Paine *gets up and joins* **Mrs Blake** *in the doorway.* **Blake** *just sits staring into space.*

Mrs Blake (*to* **Paine**) Robert's his brother. He died a few years ago. He'd been living with us. It was quite unexpected. Bill was heartbroken. When Robert died he saw his spirit ascending into the air, clapping his hands with joy . . .

Blake 'Excess of sorrow laughs. Excess of sorrow . . . weeps.'

Paine *and* **Mrs Blake** *go in.* **Blake** *turns to the audience.*

Blake I'm not usually so emotional. So *volatile.* (*He blows his nose.*) I mean, people usually get the impression that I'm a *steady* sort of fellow, with a mystical turn of mind and an actually *discernible* halo. I'm often rather sorry to disappoint them. What such people don't take into account is that our identities are never constant. We're changing all the time. From the cradle to the grave. When people are young they want to overthrow what's gone before, but when they're old they want to confine *everything* with laws. They want to bind and snare and trap!

There is a knock on the outer door.

Their *inner* conservatism creates a *political* conservatism which in turn creates the iron authoritarianism of our present society! And the stifling . . . . choking . . . *unfairness* of it all! I have personified this force and given it a human form. His name is *Urizen*! He's the old man with the white beard I was talking about earlier.

Another heavy knock at the door. **Blake** *goes to answer it.*

Who then can destroy him? Is there *anyone*? Anyone at all? The question is not rhetorical. For I have also conceived another figure in everlasting opposition to the former. Youthful! Fiery! Sparks flying from his bright red hair! *Orc*. The demon of ungovernableness! The spirit of *revolution*!

Blake *goes to the door. The stage is empty for a while. Then we become conscious of someone standing in the garden. A man in his mid twenties.*

He wears shirt and breeches in a nondescript grey colour. His face is very pale. He might be one of the people from the street outside, who has climbed the wall and jumped down into the garden, perhaps to steal an apple. He walks to the centre of the stage, an indistinct form.

Blake (*running back from answering the door*) Robert, is that you?

The man doesn't respond directly. He looks towards the house. And then walks towards it and goes on, through *the wall.*

Blake *goes back to bolt the door.*

If the play is performed in two halves, Act Two begins here.

The stage is empty for a while. **Mrs Blake** *appears in the doorway.*

Mrs Blake Where's he gone now? (*Pause.*) *William!* Your dinner's getting cold!

Blake (*off*) I won't be a minute!

She goes back inside.

Mrs Blake (*off*) He's just talking to someone.

Blake *reappears.*

Mrs Blake Who was at the door?

Blake Some of our 'neighbours' from up the road. I recognised a few faces but I couldn't tell you what their names were. There's a meeting, apparently, at the Elephant and Castle . . .

Mrs Blake And?

Blake I could see that some of them were carrying sticks and one of them had an iron bar in his hand. 'What's it all about?' I enquired. There was a bit of a silence and then one of them said, 'Politics, Mr Blake,' with a grin going up one side of his face . . . and off they went.

Mrs Blake *goes up to her husband and embraces him.*

Mrs Blake Perhaps we should ask Mr Paine to stay the night. It's not safe for him to walk back into London on his own.

Blake Are there sheets on the spare bed?

Mrs Blake I don't think so. I'll see to it in a minute.

Blake 'There's a serpent coiled in his heart. A punishment for those who write prophetic . . .'

Mrs Blake *What*?

Blake That's what Robert said.

Mrs Blake Robert?

Blake He was here a short while ago.

Mrs Blake I know.

Blake And that's what he said to me.

Mrs Blake About what?

Blake It's a warning.

Mrs Blake A warning? Who for?

Blake Our guest.

Mrs Blake Oh.

Blake He also had a vision of him in a cell no bigger than a child's grave . . . his hands and feet cut off.

Mrs Blake That's horrible! Truly *awful*! Is that what's going to happen?

Blake It's a possibility. If you imagine the future as a series of forking paths . . . then at the end of one of those paths lies the future Robert saw. But there are many other futures . . . some even more terrible.

Mrs Blake You mustn't tell him.

Blake I won't. Not directly.

Paine *wanders out from the kitchen, a plate in his hand.*

Paine Hello . . .

Mrs Blake Promise me. Promise me you won't tell him.

Blake I promise.

Paine (*mopping his forehead with a handkerchief*) It's a bit hot in there. (**Pause**.) Is anything the matter?

Blake No no. There were some people at the door. Nothing very important.

Slightly awkward pause.

I was just thinking, it's such a lovely evening. Why don't we eat out here?

Paine Why not indeed . . . what a splendid idea. Such beautiful weather . . . (*Going back into the kitchen.*) What shall I bring through?

Mrs Blake (*hurrying after him*) You sit down, Tom . . . I'll do it.

Paine (*off*) No, I insist! (**Mrs Blake** *goes in.*) Look, I'm perfectly capable of – No please! Let me – let me bring the pie.

Mrs Blake (*off*) You'll need a cloth. The dish is hot.

Paine (*off*) *Ah!* . . . Yes, you're right.

Mrs Blake (*off*) You just take your own plate through. *And* your glass. I'll bring the rest.

Paine (*off*) Oh, very well.

Paine *appears carrying his plate, the brandy bottle and a glass. He sets everything down on the table. Examines his hand. Blows on it.*

Blake Burnt yourself!

Paine No, not really. (*Shakes his hand.*)

Mrs Blake (*hurrying on with a plate of food*) Here's yours, Bill. (*Setting the food in front of him.*) It'll get cold.

Blake *just stares at it.*

Mrs Blake (*with a hint of the old lady she will become*) I have the devil's own job getting him to eat sometimes, Tom. When he's

got his head in the clouds, he'll go for days without so much
as a crust of bread. . . . Would you like a little more?

Paine No thank you, I'm very nearly full. Thank you all
the same.

Mrs Blake *goes into the kitchen.*

Blake When we were first married, we agreed to share
everything, as *equal* partners – the one should never be a
slave to the other, and so on – but as the years've gone by,
I have become increasingly absorbed in my *imagined* world
leaving Catherine to do more than her share of the drudgery.
. . . On the question of matrimonial rights we seem to have
backslid somewhat.

Mrs Blake *returns from the kitchen with her own plate, almost bumping
into* **Blake***, who is going in.*

Blake I'll bring the wine.

Mrs Blake And bring some water too.

Paine I was very young when I married. Too young I'm
afraid. We weren't together for very long. She died. I was
very bitter for a while. It seemed so *unfair*. One's feelings at
that age are particularly intense, are they not? I walked out
on my second wife. I couldn't 'settle down' . . . I still can't.
I suppose what I need is a *companion* really more than a wife.
Living as I do . . .

Blake *has returned with the wine jar quickly enough to hear most of
this. He fills up* **Paine***'s glass with brandy. And then pours wine into
his own glass.*

Mrs Blake You'll never be in one place for long enough, I
expect.

Paine (*smiling*) Long enough for what?

Mrs Blake A lasting relationship. . . . If you had to choose
between your *own* happiness and the happiness of a whole
society of people, I suppose you'd choose the people, wouldn't
you?

Paine Assuming I couldn't find a way of doing both, yes I
would. Unless of course, and with *due respect*, yours is a false

question . . . and my own 'happiness', as you call it, is *only*
to be found in . . . in an all-consuming . . . almost *exclusive*
relationship with the people . . . *generally* . . .

Mrs Blake What?

Paine I don't know. I don't know. We're talking about
something so *important*, so *personal*, how can I be precise?
Nothing's ever that clear cut anyway. Contradiction is at our
very heart.

Blake (*quietly*)
>   Once meek and in a perilous path,
>   The just man kept his course along
>   The vale of death.
>   Roses are planted where thorns grow,
>   And on the barren heath,
>   Sing the honey bees.

Paine When I first landed in America, I was taken off the
boat in a fever. My life in the new world had ended almost
before it had begun. I remember very little about it . . . except
this dream . . .

Mrs Blake *stifles a yawn.*

I was standing in a vast desert landscape, I could see for
hundreds, *thousands* of miles in every direction. The air was
still and heavy, loaded, as it were, with pestilence and death.
Clouds rolled round the sun. Thunder sounded in the sky like
artillery. And as I –

Mrs Blake (*hovering over him*) Would you like some apple
pie?

Paine Just a touch, I'm really rather full – and as I watched,
it all began to *change*. I saw that the world was on fire! I ran
from the destruction and hid in a cave. And *in the dream* I
dreamed I slept . . . and when I woke, I could see that the
air was purged and the sickly land had recovered to new life.
. . . What I had dreaded as an evil had become a blessing.

Blake I once dreamed I was on the forefinger of God as he
rewrote history . . . but yours is better.

Mrs Blake *hovers over* **Blake***'s seat with the custard.*

Blake A true vision. (*Pause.*) Tell me something – why did you not stay in America? Why did you come back to England?

Paine In a sense, I think I had outstayed my welcome. During the – no custard thank you – during the revolution I was indispensable. But *afterwards*, I don't think they were entirely sorry to see me go.

Blake The revolutionary spark burns in you too brightly, I fear. It blinds the fainter hearted.

Mrs Blake *is hovering again to collect his plate.*

Paine If I contain a *spark*, then I have met those in France who contain within themselves great *furnaces* of revolution! Their rhetoric is like – (*As* **Mrs Blake** *takes his plate.*) Delicious thank you – like the breath of dragons burning up whole fields of more timid opinion!

Blake Is Robespierre such a man?

Pause.

Paine No sir, he is *ice*.

Mrs Blake *takes the plates away to wash them.*

Blake Ice and fire do not mix.

Paine (*unable to resist scoring a point*) *Exactly!* They cancel each other out. Or more precisely, the one acts as a restraint upon the other. This is how a balance is maintained in the Assembly.

Blake But if – as you say – one faction exactly cancels out the other, there can be no progress. Only inertia. And conversely, if one faction *predominates* at the expense of the other, and seeks to *extinguish* the other . . . what then?

Paine Then you have a return to tyranny, Mr Blake.

Blake And the wheel has turned full circle . . .

Paine I can best respond to *that*, I think, by repeating what I said in a recent – not entirely unknown – publication, that 'What we now see in the world, from the revolutions of America and France, is a renovation of the *Natural Order* of things . . .'

by which I mean, 'The natural and imprescriptable rights of man . . . Liberty, Property. And resistance of oppression.'

Blake If I might quote from a recent – and almost entirely *unknown* – publication of my own:

> My mother bore me in the southern wild,
> And I am black, but oh my soul is white.

Paine Would that be a reference to the evil of slavery, Mr Blake?

Blake

> White as an angel is the English child
> But I am black as if bereaved of light.

Paine Very well, Mr Blake . . . very well. This much I'll concede: despite all *my* efforts and the efforts of a great many like-minded Americans, there is nothing in the constitution which *guarantees all* of the people their natural rights. Nevertheless. *Nevertheless!* The revolutions of America and France are the only events of any meaning in the entire century! That is *my* opinion, Mr Blake! And what is yours?

The sound of people shouting at a distance.

Mrs Blake What's that noise?

Paine I didn't hear anything. (*To* **Blake**.) Did you?

Blake *climbs the tree to investigate.*

Mrs Blake It sounded like people shouting.

Blake There's a fire blazing on One Tree Hill.

Paine Dangerously so?

Blake Don't worry. We're safe enough. It's miles away. (*He looks in a different direction.*) And there's *another* fire over there. I can't see much because of the smoke. No, it's *torches*, I think, men with torches . . .

Mrs Blake Whereabouts are they?

Blake It's hard to tell. In the general direction of the Elephant and Castle.

Paine The bringing together of men and torches, under cover of darkness, has never boded well for the rest of society, Mr Blake.

Blake Men with torches you say?

Paine That's right.

Blake You disapprove of such demonstrations?

Paine I do, yes.

Blake And what of those men who 'demonstrate' in order to 'revolutionise' society, Mr Paine?

Paine They would, I am sure, have the decency to assemble in the *daylight*, Mr Blake.

Blake *climbs down.*

Blake There are men on the streets tonight who, were they to apprehend you, would quite cheerfully hang you from the nearest tree. You *are* aware of that?

Paine I am.

Blake Public feeling is very much against you, is it not?

Paine I fear that is an understatement. (*He laughs.*)

Blake Does this not give you cause for concern?

Paine It would seem that people have a pretty low opinion of me, it's true . . . and if I believed that this was representative of the true feelings of the people, yes, there would be cause for grave concern. But since I know that this adverse opinion is very much a creation of the government, something they have gone to a great deal of time and trouble to 'manufacture', no, I am not unduly depressed.

Mrs Blake *returns from the kitchen with a steaming mug in her hand.*

Mrs Blake Tea . . .

The two men are now beginning to square up to each other. The feeling between them is no longer very friendly. We should feel that they've been holding back until now.

Blake You're not one of those people who believe that society is *conspiring* against them, are you?

Paine No, I most certainly am not.

Blake You see . . . I think *I* might be.

Paine Well *I'm* not.

Blake I didn't say you were.

Paine Not in so many words.

Blake I said '*I* might be' . . .

Paine All right, *you* 'might be' but *I'm* not!

Blake It's a tendency on my part which has to be resisted . . . I think.

Paine Not on mine!

Blake All right. All right. All that I am saying *is* . . . it's painful when people reject your work. It's hard to admit to yourself that your work might not be very good. And it's very tempting sometimes to think that there might be *other* reasons for that fact . . . reasons outside of *oneself*. . . . Do you see what I'm saying?

Paine Yes, I think I do. But that's not true in my case. . . . Don't you realise . . . people are being *actively* encouraged to *hate* me!

Blake They *are*?

Paine Public opinion has been *corrupted*! It's my belief that if people were left to decide for themselves, they wouldn't be so keen to *destroy* the very man who is trying *hardest* to *liberate* them! (*He laughs.*) It's an extremely ironic situation. Wouldn't you agree?

Blake Oh yes, yes, yes. . . . Is this mainly the work of the government, do you think? Or the king?

Paine The king? You mean personally? (**Blake** *nods.*) I don't think so. He's mad of course. They all are. It's something to do with having access to all that power. . . . It *is* true though that the king's party has the most to fear. There's no place for monarchy in my vision of a republican Britain.

Blake Would you kill the king?

Paine I'm not a bloodthirsty man. Nor am I personally vindictive. It's the *institution* of monarchy I wish to destroy, not the person of the king himself.

Blake But to get rid of the monarchy, don't you also have to get rid of the monarch too? And all his family? *All* of them . . . down to the last drop?

Paine I would hope not . . . with all my heart.

Mrs Blake It's a funny thing monarchy, isn't it? (*The two men look at her, surprised to hear another voice.*) Someone once told me about a man who wrote a letter to the American Senate, proposing himself as king – the King of America. He was from Normandy. And he had a better pedigree, he said, than William the Conqueror. So when the Americans didn't reply, he sent them *another* letter saying he'd call off the invasion if they'd give him a hundred pounds. Through the post . . . (*The men start laughing. The tension between them temporarily defused.*) Well, to cut a long story short, the Americans didn't reply to *that* letter either. And of course he never invaded. I mean, he couldn't, could he? It's much too far away for one thing . . . America . . .

Paine As a point of information, it was Benjamin Franklin who he approached with the idea, and it wasn't a hundred pounds he asked for, it was thirty thousand.

Mrs Blake How do *you* know that?

Paine The story's in my book.

Mrs Blake You mean it's *true*?

Paine It most certainly is.

Mrs Blake Well I'm blowed. . . . Which book was it in?

Paine *The Rights of Man.*

Mrs Blake *Was* it?

Pause.

Paine That's probably where you came across it . . . in the first place.

Mrs Blake No, I don't think so . . .

Paine Why not?

Pause.

Mrs Blake I can't read.

Paine Ah.

Paine *is embarrassed. He'd like to withdraw the question. The situation is tense again. A storm is brewing.*

Mrs Blake It won't be long though . . . Bill's been teaching me. . . . I can make out simple words, but I'm not very confident. Yet. 'Girls are fit for one thing,' my father used to say . . . 'And it comes *natural* so there's no need for any book learning.' And then he'd laugh, like he'd said something really funny.

Paine (*quietly*) We're going to change all that, Mrs Blake.

Mrs Blake And the sooner the better I say.

Paine We're going to turn the world upside down.

Blake (*cold, very intense*) And having done that . . . will you be content to live in an 'upside down world', Mr Paine, or will you set it back to rights?

Paine I don't understand you . . . not quite.

Blake I'm asking, I suppose, what's going to happen once the old order has been torn down? Because, unless people can thrive in a state of anarchy – which is a delightful idea in theory and such a difficult one in practice – *new* rules will have to be drafted and if necessary *enforced*! In other words, in order to *maintain* the new order, a certain amount of *coercion* is going to be required. So how can you be sure you have not torn down one form of tyranny only to replace it with another?

THE STORM BREAKS

Paine (*increasingly furious*) You *can't* be sure! You can't be *sure* of anything! Will the sun rise tomorrow? In all probability it will. But it may not! Do you have to be *absolutely sure* before you can approve of something, or more precisely *commit* to it? (*Pause.*) You see, I don't believe that you do. . . . A little while ago, we proposed a toast: 'To a better world'. We were agreed, the three of us. . . . Was that just a sentimental yearning? Lip service to the idea of progress? Not as far as I was concerned!

I can't speak for you two obviously. It's my belief that you have to *dedicate* yourself to the idea, to the *hope* that society can be changed for the better! It doesn't *do* to look too far into the future. If we could see the way ahead, if we could see the obstacles that confront us, the pitfalls, the landslides, wolves, bandits, ogres, *monsters*, perhaps we'd never set out in the first place! So let's just take one step at a time. And deal with each problem as we come to it!

Blake I'm afraid I don't see it quite like you do –

Paine That's not important! What's imp –

Blake Hear me out!

Paine What's important is that people are –

Blake Listen to me will you? I see it as a struggle –

Paine – are given a –

Blake (*shouting now*) A struggle, an *everlasting* struggle between two contradictory forces! I had the good grace to hear you out, Mr Paine, surely you can do the same for me. A *struggle* between the state and those who would destroy the state, which neither side can really win! Look at it this way – imagine a desert. A red sun in a slate grey sky. Two figures locked in combat. Their feet kicking up clouds of dust. One of the figures is old. He has a long white beard. And tearing at his throat is a young man, sparks flying from his flaming hair. Sometimes the old man gets the upper hand. Sometimes the young man. But neither can *triumph* over the other!

Pause.

Paine Finished?

Pause.

Blake Yes.

Paine Very well. . . . Can I just say that I see the point you're making and I'd really rather not dispute it with you, if it's all the same to you.

Blake Why not?

Paine Why not? Because it isn't relevant, that's why not! What *you think* is of great concern to *you* I'm sure, as it is to any *individual*! But it doesn't really affect the issue . . . *that* . . . by far the vast majority of people in this country are born into a society where they are *deprived* of their natural *rights*! And all your symbolic imaginings and metaphysical objections – interesting as they are in themselves – don't impinge on that fact one little bit! We're living in a society which practises the enslavement of children, for God's sake! A starving man can be hanged for poaching a rabbit! I needn't go on. You know what I'm talking about! We need a *written* constitution which guarantees people their natural rights! So that every man has a house to live in, and work to do – *proper* work – and food to eat. So that every man – and every woman too – can be cared for when they're sick and looked after when they're old. So that every man can have a share in the running of his country, by voting into office a Member of Parliament of his choice and not some posturing *ninny* imposed on him from the ranks of the ruling elite! That's what I'm talking about! I'm not interested in philosophical *niceties*! I'm interested in *practicalities*! *What* do we do? *When* do we do it? And *how*! I've been called a firebrand! A fanatic! A traitor! A devil! Now that seems just a bit of an overstatement to me. I'm a fairly ordinary and above all *reasonable* man. And I want the country to be governed in a *reasonable* way. And that's all I want. But if that means turning the world upside down, then I'm the man to do it! And if it then entails taking the world by the ankles and giving it a God-almighty *shake*, then by jumping Jesus I'll do that too!

Long pause.

Blake (*through gritted teeth*) Can I just ask you one question?

Paine Do.

Blake It's not an easy question to frame, so bear with me.

Paine Right-i-ho.

Blake Our *understanding* of the world is clouded by our feelings, our desires, fears, frustrations and so on, wouldn't you agree? I mean it's very difficult to see the world – *society*, rather – as it really is . . .

Paine Is it?

Blake Let me give you an example: a man has grown timid and subservient because he was beaten as a child. This behaviour persists into adult life, even after the death of his parents. Whenever he's confronted by a 'representative of the state' he *cringes*. This is because he's expecting the state to behave like his vengeful family. He has the one confused with the other.

Paine Go on.

Blake *So* – and this is the question I want to ask you – how can we be sure it's *society* we're changing and not some unhappy aspect of ourselves? Because (*without giving* **Paine** *time to answer*) anyone who leads the people into revolution has to be free of such delusions. Otherwise, in imposing his will on to the nation he will inadvertently *subdue* it! Letting loose whole tribes of inner demons which will arise shrieking from the top of his head to torment and enslave the people all over again! I can imagine the future as a succession of tyrannies, each one subtler than the one before, stretching like a line of gibbets into infinity! No. Before we can commit ourselves to revolutions there must first be *revelations*! Men must know themselves. Be in harmony with themselves – enlightened and full of the holy spirit – before they can presume to know what is best for their fellow men.

Paine I thought you were asking me a question.

Blake It got lost rather.

Paine I'll say . . . (*Pause.*) I'd no idea you were such a 'conservative', Mr Blake.

Blake Excuse me, Mr Paine, but my heart quite outran my head. . . . I *approve* of revolution – the revolutions of America and France have my undying support – but that doesn't make me *uncritical*. Particularly of the bloodshed.

Paine I thought you were asking me a question.

Blake As I say . . . it got lost.

We hear the sound of people shouting in the street, indistinct at first.

Paine I think I can provide an answer, nonetheless.

Blake That's very civil of you.

Paine Think nothing of it. Your attitude reminds me of a certain African bird, which in order to escape from the lions of that continent, is inclined to insert its head into the desert sand; it is thereby unable to perceive the pursuing lions and mistakenly concludes that it has successfully eluded the ripping teeth and hungry jaws. When the people rise up against the state, they'll be engaged in a bloody battle! There'll be no time for finer feelings and personal revelations! And it's *unrealistic* to suppose anything else! Such an attitude – as the one you've just described – puts *personal* morality before *public* concern and thereby puts the *individual* above the common herd. It leads to non-action. Inertia. Contemplation. Mysticism. Can't you see? It's drawing you away from the world ever deeper into *yourself*!

Blake How beautiful it is tonight. Look at the sky. The constellation of Orion. The moon and the fixed stars. The planets in their orbits. The North Star and the Plough. But when I shut my eyes . . . (*He shuts them.*) It's just the same . . . I see the *same* universe *inside* myself as well. I'm a poet you see . . .

Paine Ah . . . that explains it.

Blake I know it's a terrible job, but someone has to do it. You know it, of course, from an early age. You have this *compulsion*. You can't help it. And what does it mean, this 'being a poet'? Well, for one thing, your commitment isn't towards *action*, it's more – No. Look at it this way. People may not like what you're saying, they may not even *understand* what you're saying, but at least they know they're not being swindled or deluded. A poet who tells lies simply isn't a poet. There's something deep inside, a cussed thing which will brook no compromise. So that when the time comes – *as it will* – and it's important that you *speak out* clearly and honestly, you will have earned the right to be believed! Not as a politician is believed, which is to say hardly at all, or a mere pamphleteer, but as a true poet speaking with a *prophetic voice*!

Paine (*shouting now*) And what might that be, Mr Blake? The 'prophetic voice'? It's so seldom heard these days. If at all. . . . Let's be realistic for a moment shall we? Speaking as a 'mere' pamphleteer, it seems to me that you 'poets' have a somewhat inflated idea of your own importance. You say that your commitment is towards *truth* not *action*. . . . You know what I say? NONSENSE! That's what I say! Nothing so high flown I'm afraid, your commitment is primarily to *yourself*! To your

talent! Your art! Otherwise you'd be 'merely' interested in the
people *for their own sake*! And 'merely' involved in the process
of giving them back their due! You're like some terrible sort
of . . . *engine*, designed to process experience, devouring it at
one end and farting it out, nicely illustrated, at the other!
All *this*. (*Waving his arms about.*) It's just grist to your mill,
isn't it? *Listen!* The times are too critical for that sort of
self indulgence! Maybe if people of *your* sensibility stopped
thinking of yourselves as 'artists' first and foremost, we might
get somewhere!

Blake (*raging mad, eyes half shut. Screaming quietly*)

> What is the price of experience? do men buy it for a
>   song?
> Or wisdom for a dance in the street? No, it is bought with
>   the price
> Of all that a man hath, his house, his wife, his children,
> Wisdom is sold in the desolate market where none come
>   to buy
> And the with'rd field where the farmer ploughs for bread
>   in vain.

*The mob are now in the street outside. We slowly become aware of their
murmuring and shuffling.*

Blake *jumps on the table.*

> It is an easy thing to triumph in the summer sun,
> And in the vintage and to sing on the wagon loaded with
>   corn.
> It is an easy thing to talk of patience to the afflicted,
> To speak the laws of prudence to the homeless wanderer,
> To listen to the hungry raven's cry in the wintry season
> When the red blood is filled with wine and the marrow of
>   lambs.

There is a hesitant knock on the door. **Blake** *doesn't hear it.*

> Then the groan and the dolour are quite forgotten, and
>   the slave grinding at the mill,
> And the captive in chains, and the poor in prison, and
>   the soldier in the field
> Where the shattered bone hath laid him groaning among
>   the happier dead.

Another knock on the door. **Mrs Blake** *goes to answer it.*

It is an easy thing to rejoice in the tents of prosperity:
Thus could I sing and thus rejoice. But it is not so
    with me!

Silence.

Paine *pours himself a brandy. He has almost finished the bottle.* **Blake**
sits, abstracted.

Paine Can I help you to a glass of apple wine?

Blake No. Thank you.

Pause.

Paine Are those torches outside? Or is something on fire?

Blake (*without looking*) Torches, I think.

Pause.

Paine I feel safe here. Isn't that strange? As if . . . *inside*
this garden, life is always peaceful, civilised, under a summer
sky. And *outside*, the plague is raging through dirty streets and
naked men are cutting each other's throats.

Blake *doesn't answer. There is a 'thump' as a missile hits the side of
the house.*

Blake Don't be too sure.

Paine Your wife's out there.

Blake What?

Paine Kate. She's –

Blake She's what?

Paine She's out there. She went to answer the door.

Blake *Did* she?

Paine She's talking to them I expect.

Blake Talking to *who*?

Paine Whoever it is.

Blake She's *out* there you say?

Paine Yes.

Blake Why didn't you tell me?

Paine I did!

Blake Sorry, I didn't realise.

A muffled cry from the street.

Paine Perhaps we'd better –

Blake No, stay where you are.

He walks purposefully towards the outer door, almost bumping into **Mrs Blake** *on her way back.*

Blake Are you all right?

Mrs Blake *Me?* I'm fine. They don't scare *me* . . . roughs like that . . . they're all piss and wind. . . . Thought they could intimidate me. Ha! I soon gave 'em what for!

She pours out a large glass of apple wine and knocks it back.

Ah, that's better. . . . I recognised one of them, from down our way in Battersea. A thin spidery little bloke called Sam Boscow. He used to sit on his front steps all day pulling the wings, of beetles. He hasn't changed. Thick as two short planks, just like the rest of them. . . . I'll tell you something, Mr Paine . . . you've got a job on with that lot.

Blake What did they want?

Mrs Blake 'What brings you lot out on the streets?' I said. 'We're after them dirty republican bastards,' one of them replied. If worms had faces, that's what *his* was like – half blind and crumpled up. 'We're going to tar and feather 'em!' he said. 'And where are you going to get tar from at this time of night?' I said. There was a bit of a pause and then he said, 'None of your business!' and bared his teeth at me like a monkey. 'We're not safe in our beds!' this little man shouted and he threw something into the garden.

Paine Yes, we heard it.

Mrs Blake Then this woman who I half recognised came up to me, one of our neighbours from up the road, one of the ones you talked about earlier, I shouldn't be at all surprised. 'We saw someone entering this building tonight,' she said, implying all sorts of horrible things. 'We know what sort of company *you* keep.' She was so close to me, I could see these patches of rouge on her cheeks. 'And what's it to you?' I said, knowing her now for a whore, 'I don't come knocking on *your* door, do I? Checking what sort of company *you* keep.' She backed off at that. 'Let us in!' the little man shouted. 'We want to search the place!' 'Over my dead body!' I said and slammed the door in his face!

Paine Bravely said, Kate. Well done.

Mrs Blake It was nothing really. It takes a woman to stand up to them.

Blake Is the door secure?

Mrs Blake I put the bar across.

Paine Are they dispersing do you think?

Mrs Blake It's hard to tell.

There is a horrible low laugh from the street.

Mrs Blake Get away home! Or I'll call out the Watch!

An indistinct noise from the street.

Paine What did they say?

Mrs Blake Sounded to me like, 'We *are* the Watch.' Or something like that.

Paine Shall we go inside?

Mrs Blake No, we'll stay put. I don't want them trampling all over the garden. Out here we can keep an eye on them.

Paine You seem to be taking things very lightly, I must say . . .

Mrs Blake Don't worry about them. They're just . . . *pathetic*.

Blake (*more concerned than* **Mrs Blake**) Did you put the sheets on the spare bed?

Mrs Blake *What?* Oh no . . . I clean forgot. I'll do it now.

Blake No. You sit down. I've got some prints drying in there. I'll sort it out in a minute.

Mrs Blake The sheets are in the linen press. In *our* room.

Blake Right.

Mrs Blake Use the *flannel* ones. They're in the second drawer down. *Don't* use the – Oh *I'll* do it.

Blake No, *I'll* do it. (*He gets up.*) The flannel ones did you say – ?

Mrs Blake Yes. The linen ones need mending.

Paine Don't put yourself out on my account. I have every intention –

There is another noise from the street. A muffled shout and a giggle. **Blake** *stops in his tracks.*

Blake (*shouting*). What's going on?

A brief silence. Then a 'crash' as a brick goes through a window.

Blake Break my windows would you? Break another and I'll be out there breaking a few heads!

Mrs Blake *Bill!*

Blake *makes a run for the outer door.*

Blake (*off*) That's right . . . turn tail then, you yellow-bellied bastards! Bloody typical!

Mrs Blake He's mustard when he's roused.

Paine So it would seem.

Blake *returns.*

Blake They've gone . . . chased down the street by the angel of death. They didn't see him at first. He was hiding in a cloud. Then he flew past me, raising his sword in his right hand.

Paine, *not for the first time this evening, is at a loss. He doesn't know if* **Blake** *is telling the truth in a symbolic sort of way, or actually recounting a vision. Nor, for that matter, do we.*

Paine Quite an eventful evening . . . one way and another.

Mrs Blake I'll say.

Paine I have never before, experienced so much so quickly.

Mrs Blake That's Bill for you . . . (*Pause.*) He's always upsetting people.

Paine I'm not 'upset' exactly.

Mrs Blake I don't mean in a bad sort of way. I mean . . . well, this woman came round once. I can't remember her name. She was very highly strung. Tall and thin with protruding teeth. And *freckles*. About forty. I don't think Bill really took to her, he didn't say a word to her all evening. Then just as she was about to leave, he whispered something in her ear. She was so overcome she quite lost the use of her legs and we had to sit her in a wheelbarrow and push her all the way home. (*She laughs.*)

Paine *laughs politely.* **Blake** *stares at the ground.*

Mrs Blake Are you two still friends?

Paine I very much hope so.

Blake 'Opposition is true friendship.'

Paine Well . . . (*He stands.*) That's one way of putting it.

Blake Do you have a better?

Paine (*offering his hand*) I'm very pleased to have met you, Mr Blake. It's been a pleasure talking to you.

Mrs Blake You're not going are you?

Blake (*shaking his hand*) Are we still not on first name terms, Mr Paine?

Paine It would seem *not*, Mr Blake. Perhaps when we meet again . . . we'll be sufficiently at ease to drop the formality . . .

Blake That may never happen.

Blake *walks away frowning.*

Mrs Blake There's a spare bed upstairs, if you'd like to stay.

Paine That's very kind of you, but no, thank you.

Mrs Blake I just have to change the sheets, it won't take a minute.

Paine No, please . . . I must get back tonight. I have things to do.

Mrs Blake It's no trouble.

Paine Thanks all the same, Kate. But I have to go to a meeting. In the city . . . in about an hour's time. . . . People are expecting me.

Blake A meeting?

Paine Yes . . . I'm giving a bit of a talk.

Mrs Blake But it's not *safe* out there. There's some desperate people on the streets.

Paine Footpads and bloody-bones . . . I know.

Mrs Blake And *worse*! It's not safe! Particularly for *you*! You're a marked man! And it's such a long walk back into London. You'd be better off staying the night in my opinion and setting off in the morning when it's light.

Paine I'll be on my way, thanks all the same. (*He stands, looking for his coat.*) I realise there are some fairly unpleasant types about . . . and perhaps I should be frightened of them. But I'm not. . . . Funny isn't it? Have you seen my coat anywhere?

Mrs Blake You've been sitting on it.

Paine Ah. (*He straightens the coat and puts it on.*) You see, I think to myself . . . all I have to do is *talk* to them and they'll see reason. It's sheer arrogance of course and it doesn't always work out. Last year when I was in France. One dark night I was apprehended by the mob and jostled about a bit. I kept saying, 'I'm on your side,' but that made very little difference as none of them spoke any English and I had no French. When I ran for it, they assumed I was telling lies and laid about me with their sticks. . . . There's a moral there somewhere: always learn the language of the country that you're living in . . . and never run away. Where's my hat?

Mrs Blake But this is *England*! And you're not running *away*.

Blake It's on the window sill.

Paine Thank you. (*He gets the hat and puts it on.*)

Mrs Blake You don't have to *prove* anything to them, you know.

Paine I know.

Pause.

Mrs Blake You're going over London Bridge?

Paine I expect so.

Mrs Blake How will you get there? Along the riverside?

Paine I *could* go that way, yes.

Mrs Blake Take care, won't you.

Paine *kisses her goodbye.*

Paine Thank you for supper . . . I realise you only cooked for two. I hope the act of sharing it . . . didn't prove too much of a sacrifice . . .

Mrs Blake Get away with you.

Paine I'm very happy to have made your acquaintance.

He moves hesitantly towards the outer door. **Blake** *is still seated, staring at the floor.*

Paine Goodbye, Mr Blake.

Blake (*looking up*) Why did you come?

Paine What?

Blake You just *arrived*. Without warning. You haven't said why.

Paine (*winking at* **Mrs Blake**) I came to see you.

Blake Why?

Paine To talk.

Blake I see.

Paine *doesn't want to talk to* **Blake** *about his fearful run through the streets. Not at this moment. Throughout the following he keeps glancing towards* **Mrs Blake,** *willing her not to bring up the subject.*

Paine It's so rare to meet someone with whom one might share an opinion . . . don't you think?

No response from **Blake**.

It's surprising that we haven't met before, actually . . . at one of Mr Johnson's little get-togethers. The thing is . . . we never seem to have turned up on the same night . . . otherwise we'd've met long before. No. What I thought *was* . . . I really ought to make an effort and *meet* you, before I – What am I saying? Before I *what*?

Blake Leave the country.

Paine Leave the –

Blake Forget about meetings. Leave the country. (*Pause.*) If you don't, you're a dead man.

Paine (*at length*) Aren't you overstating th –

Blake LEAVE THE COUNTRY! Do it tonight! Pack your things and go! (**Blake** *gets up and takes his hand.*) They want to silence you, Mr Paine. They'll use any means. They'll kill you if they have to. It's important that you go on speaking out. Leave the country! Go to France. Speak out from there.

Paine (*shaking his hand again*) Thank you for your advice. I'll give it every consideration.

Blake Don't hesitate. *Go!*

Paine *wanders towards the outer door.*

Paine I enjoyed our chat.

Blake Yes . . . very stimulating.

Paine Very. (*Pause.*) One thing . . .

Blake Yes?

Paine When I arrived . . .

Blake Yes?

Paine When we shook hands rather . . . you were both of you . . . naked.

Blake We were . . . yes.

Paine WHY?

Blake Why not? (*He smiles.*)

Paine (*smiling*) I always thought you were a religious man, Mr Blake.

Blake Oh I am . . . *very.*

Paine I have to say, that I've seen very little evidence of it.

Blake God is within.

Paine *Within.* Ah . . . that would explain it. Bye.

He goes.

Mrs Blake That was a very nice evening. All things considered. He's such a pleasant gentleman, don't you think? And such an accomplished talker. Mmm. It got a little *animated* there for a minute, didn't it? Still. You've always enjoyed a good scrap.

She goes into the kitchen with her plate and **Paine**'s *plate. She leaves* **Blake**'s *plate, as there is still a large amount of pie uneaten.*

Blake *rapidly climbs the tree. He stares out in the direction* **Paine** *has taken.*

Mrs Blake (*returning from the kitchen*) Before tonight I'd always thought of him as a fanatic – terribly intense with a wild expression. You know. But he's not like that at all, is he? (*Collecting the glasses.*) He seems so *reasonable* . . . and he's got such nice eyes . . . and such a friendly face. . . . He's not my idea of a bogey-man, is he y – Bill, where are you?

Blake I'm up here.

Mrs Blake That's a relief. For a moment I thought you were chasing off after him.

Blake No . . .

Mrs Blake What are you doing up there?

Blake Just looking . . .

Mrs Blake You didn't finish your pie.

No response.

Mrs Blake Shall I save it for later? Or won't you be hungry?

She picks up the empty brandy bottle and the wine jar.

Mrs Blake You were a bit silly buying all this. We haven't a penny for tomorrow.

Blake *climbs down.*

Blake I'm owed some for that last lot of prints. I'll go and see about it in the morning.

Mrs Blake And make sure you do.

She goes into the kitchen.

Blake *sits under the tree. After a while he takes out a pipe and plays a tune. It is in a minor key with an odd halting rhythm.*

The music seems to get louder.

The lights fade until only **Blake** *is lit. Around him the stage is dark.*

There is a fluttering sound from above. **Blake** *stops playing and looks up.*

High in the trees, there is an angel. *Naked, with golden hair and silvery wings. It should be seen in a natural position, with its back, perhaps, to the audience.*

The audience gets the briefest of glimpses, before the lights snap out!